The Loch Ness Mystery

Written by Sarah Rice

Illustrated by Monica Auriemma

Collins

Have you heard the mystery of Loch Ness?
Thousands of tourists visit this Scottish loch every year to photograph it and catch a glimpse of what lurks beneath the waves.

They are all searching for the Loch Ness Monster.

Loch Ness is a large, deep lake in the Scottish Highlands.

Fact!
Loch is the Scottish word for lake.

The mystery of the Loch Ness Monster began over a thousand years ago. A man called Saint Columba claimed he encountered a strange creature in the loch.

The story became prominent in the 1930s, when tourists said they saw a creature with a large body, wavy neck and skin like an elephant.

Fact!
The Loch Ness Monster
is also called Nessie.

9

In 1934, a photograph was captured by a surgeon called Robert Wilson. It showed the creature's head and neck emerging from the murky depths.

11

Analysis of the photograph showed it was a hoax —
it was not a real monster.

It was actually a plastic
head on a toy boat.

13

The surgeon's photograph was fake, but other people have allegedly spotted the monster in the loch.

What could it be?

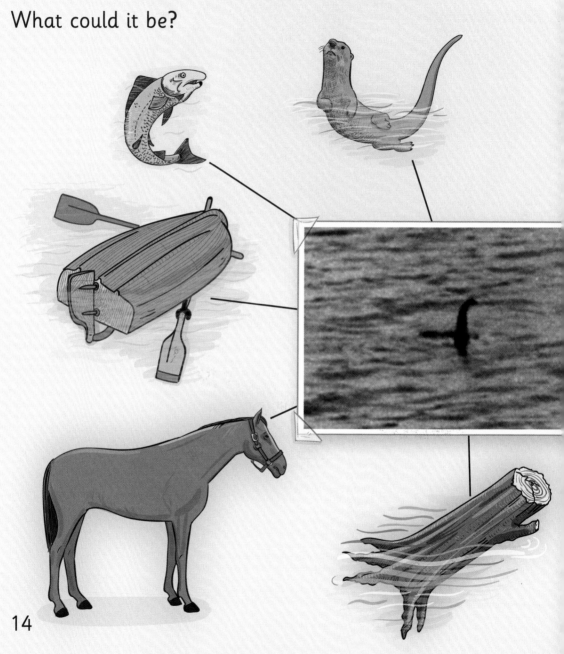

From the 1970s, extensive searches of the loch were conducted using sonar beams to catch images of objects.

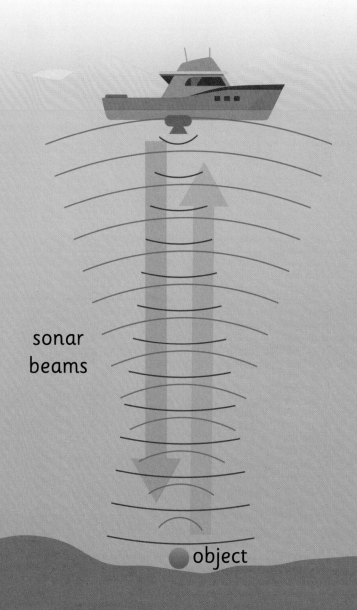

sonar beams

object

In 1975, a large object was captured on screen, but researchers couldn't confirm whether it was the monster.

In 2018, biologists from around the world tested samples from Loch Ness. Their analysis continues to help us understand what lives in the loch.

Fact!
These biologists study life under lakes and seas.

No photographs or sightings of Nessie have been confirmed.

However, interest in the phenomenon of a monster in the loch continues.

Timeline

1000 years ago

1930s

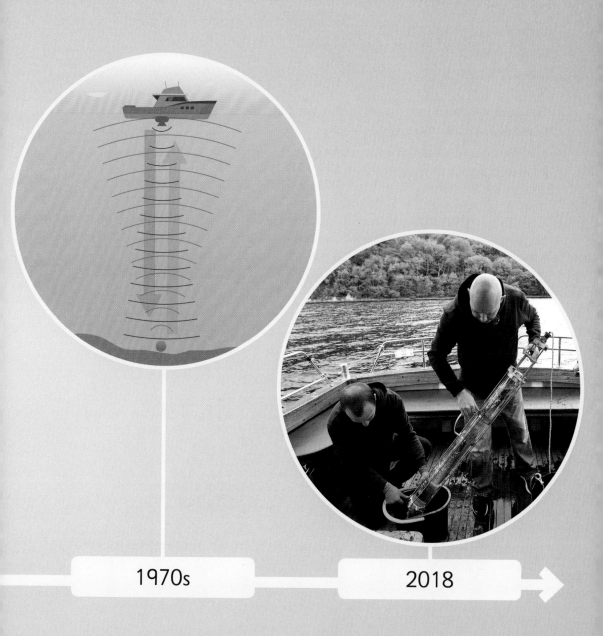

1970s

2018

After reading

Letters and Sounds: Phase 5

Word count: 300

Focus phonemes: /v/ ve /j/ g, ge /c/ ch /ee/ y, e /f/ ph /ch/ tch, t /w/ wh /igh/ y /l/ le /s/ se

Common exception words: of, to, the, are, said, were, their, people

Curriculum links: Science; Geography

National Curriculum learning objectives: Spoken language: use relevant strategies to build their vocabulary; use spoken language to develop understanding through speculating, hypothesising, imagining and exploring ideas; Reading/word reading: respond speedily with the correct sound to graphemes (letters or groups of letters) for all 40+ phonemes, including, where applicable, alternative sounds for graphemes; Reading/comprehension: understand both the books they can already read accurately and fluently and those they listen to by drawing on what they already know or on background information and vocabulary provided by the teacher; discuss the significance of the title

Developing fluency

- Your child may enjoy hearing you read the book.
- Model reading the first two pages with lots of expression and interest about the mystery of the Loch Ness Monster.
- Now ask your child to read pages 6 and 7 or 8 and 9 to you using lots of expression to tell you about the history of the Loch Ness Monster.

Phonic practice

- Ask your child what this letter sound is: /j/. Say it together a few times.
- Now read page 4 to your child. Ask them to listen out for the letter sound /j/. When they hear it, ask them to repeat the word to you. (*large*)
- Look at the word **large** together. Ask your child which letters stand for the letter sound /j/. (*ge*)
- Now do the same thing with page 10. (*surgeon, emerging*)

Extending vocabulary

- Read page 2 again. Ask your child if they can think of another word that could be used instead of **lurks**. (e.g. *hides*) Now ask them if they can think of another word that could be used instead of **glimpse**. (e.g. *view, sight*)